50 Chia Pudding for a Healthy Start Recipes

By: Kelly Johnson

Table of Contents

- Classic Vanilla Chia Pudding
- Chocolate Almond Chia Pudding
- Mango Coconut Chia Pudding
- Peanut Butter Banana Chia Pudding
- Strawberry Almond Chia Pudding
- Matcha Green Tea Chia Pudding
- Blueberry Lemon Chia Pudding
- Coconut Lime Chia Pudding
- Pumpkin Spice Chia Pudding
- Cherry Vanilla Chia Pudding
- Raspberry Coconut Chia Pudding
- Cinnamon Apple Chia Pudding
- Mocha Chia Pudding
- Pineapple Coconut Chia Pudding
- Chia Pudding Parfait with Granola
- Chocolate Coconut Chia Pudding
- Almond Joy Chia Pudding
- Kiwi Lime Chia Pudding
- Maple Pecan Chia Pudding
- Lemon Poppy Seed Chia Pudding
- Acai Berry Chia Pudding
- Banana Nut Chia Pudding
- Tropical Papaya Chia Pudding
- Chocolate Raspberry Chia Pudding
- Mixed Berry Chia Pudding
- Coconut Mango Chia Pudding
- S'mores Chia Pudding
- Pear Ginger Chia Pudding
- Sweet Potato Cinnamon Chia Pudding
- Peach Chia Pudding with Almonds
- Carrot Cake Chia Pudding
- Raspberry Chia Pudding with Walnuts
- Tropical Kiwi Chia Pudding
- Pomegranate Chia Pudding
- Cashew Butter Chia Pudding

- Lemon Raspberry Chia Pudding
- Cinnamon Roll Chia Pudding
- Avocado Chocolate Chia Pudding
- Pineapple Chia Pudding with Macadamia Nuts
- Watermelon Mint Chia Pudding
- Coffee Chia Pudding
- Papaya Lime Chia Pudding
- Chocolate Cherry Chia Pudding
- Apple Cinnamon Chia Pudding
- Spiced Pear Chia Pudding
- Blueberry Peach Chia Pudding
- Cacao Mint Chia Pudding
- Goji Berry Chia Pudding
- Hazelnut Chocolate Chia Pudding
- Fig and Walnut Chia Pudding

Classic Vanilla Chia Pudding

Ingredients:

- 1/4 cup chia seeds
- 1 cup almond milk (or any milk of choice)
- 1 tsp vanilla extract
- 1-2 tbsp maple syrup or honey
- Fresh berries or granola for topping

Instructions:

1. **Mix**: In a bowl or jar, combine chia seeds, almond milk, vanilla extract, and sweetener. Stir well to prevent clumping.
2. **Refrigerate**: Cover and refrigerate for at least 4 hours or overnight to allow the chia seeds to absorb the liquid and thicken.
3. **Serve**: Top with fresh berries or granola before serving.

Chocolate Almond Chia Pudding

Ingredients:

- 1/4 cup chia seeds
- 1 cup almond milk
- 1 tbsp cocoa powder
- 1-2 tbsp maple syrup or honey
- 1/4 tsp almond extract
- Sliced almonds and dark chocolate shavings for topping

Instructions:

1. **Mix**: In a bowl or jar, combine chia seeds, almond milk, cocoa powder, maple syrup, and almond extract. Stir well to combine.
2. **Refrigerate**: Cover and refrigerate for at least 4 hours or overnight to thicken.
3. **Serve**: Top with sliced almonds and dark chocolate shavings before serving.

Mango Coconut Chia Pudding

Ingredients:

- 1/4 cup chia seeds
- 1 cup coconut milk
- 1/2 cup mango puree (fresh or frozen)
- 1-2 tbsp maple syrup or honey
- Shredded coconut for topping

Instructions:

1. **Mix**: In a bowl or jar, combine chia seeds, coconut milk, mango puree, and sweetener. Stir well to combine.
2. **Refrigerate**: Cover and refrigerate for at least 4 hours or overnight.
3. **Serve**: Top with shredded coconut before serving.

Peanut Butter Banana Chia Pudding

Ingredients:

- 1/4 cup chia seeds
- 1 cup almond milk
- 2 tbsp peanut butter
- 1 ripe banana, mashed
- 1-2 tbsp maple syrup or honey
- Banana slices for topping

Instructions:

1. **Mix**: In a bowl or jar, combine chia seeds, almond milk, peanut butter, mashed banana, and sweetener. Stir well to combine.
2. **Refrigerate**: Cover and refrigerate for at least 4 hours or overnight.
3. **Serve**: Top with banana slices before serving.

Strawberry Almond Chia Pudding

Ingredients:

- 1/4 cup chia seeds
- 1 cup almond milk
- 1/2 cup fresh strawberries, pureed
- 1-2 tbsp maple syrup or honey
- Sliced almonds and strawberries for topping

Instructions:

1. **Mix**: In a bowl or jar, combine chia seeds, almond milk, strawberry puree, and sweetener. Stir well.
2. **Refrigerate**: Cover and refrigerate for at least 4 hours or overnight.
3. **Serve**: Top with sliced almonds and fresh strawberry slices before serving.

Matcha Green Tea Chia Pudding

Ingredients:

- 1/4 cup chia seeds
- 1 cup almond milk
- 1 tsp matcha powder
- 1-2 tbsp maple syrup or honey
- Coconut flakes or chopped nuts for topping

Instructions:

1. **Mix**: In a bowl or jar, combine chia seeds, almond milk, matcha powder, and sweetener. Stir well until the matcha powder dissolves.
2. **Refrigerate**: Cover and refrigerate for at least 4 hours or overnight.
3. **Serve**: Top with coconut flakes or chopped nuts before serving.

Blueberry Lemon Chia Pudding

Ingredients:

- 1/4 cup chia seeds
- 1 cup almond milk
- 1/2 cup blueberries (fresh or frozen)
- 1 tbsp lemon juice
- 1-2 tbsp maple syrup or honey
- Fresh blueberries and lemon zest for topping

Instructions:

1. **Mix**: In a bowl or jar, combine chia seeds, almond milk, blueberries, lemon juice, and sweetener. Stir well to combine.
2. **Refrigerate**: Cover and refrigerate for at least 4 hours or overnight.
3. **Serve**: Top with fresh blueberries and lemon zest before serving.

Coconut Lime Chia Pudding

Ingredients:

- 1/4 cup chia seeds
- 1 cup coconut milk
- 1 tbsp lime juice
- Zest of 1 lime
- 1-2 tbsp maple syrup or honey
- Shredded coconut for topping

Instructions:

1. **Mix**: In a bowl or jar, combine chia seeds, coconut milk, lime juice, lime zest, and sweetener. Stir well to combine.
2. **Refrigerate**: Cover and refrigerate for at least 4 hours or overnight.
3. **Serve**: Top with shredded coconut before serving.

Pumpkin Spice Chia Pudding

Ingredients:

- 1/4 cup chia seeds
- 1 cup almond milk
- 1/4 cup pumpkin puree
- 1/2 tsp pumpkin spice
- 1-2 tbsp maple syrup or honey
- Whipped cream or cinnamon for topping (optional)

Instructions:

1. **Mix**: In a bowl or jar, combine chia seeds, almond milk, pumpkin puree, pumpkin spice, and sweetener. Stir well.
2. **Refrigerate**: Cover and refrigerate for at least 4 hours or overnight.
3. **Serve**: Top with whipped cream or a sprinkle of cinnamon before serving.

Cherry Vanilla Chia Pudding

Ingredients:

- 1/4 cup chia seeds
- 1 cup almond milk
- 1/2 cup fresh or frozen cherries, pureed
- 1 tsp vanilla extract
- 1-2 tbsp maple syrup or honey
- Chopped cherries for topping

Instructions:

1. **Mix**: In a bowl or jar, combine chia seeds, almond milk, cherry puree, vanilla extract, and sweetener. Stir well.
2. **Refrigerate**: Cover and refrigerate for at least 4 hours or overnight.
3. **Serve**: Top with chopped cherries before serving.

Raspberry Coconut Chia Pudding

Ingredients:

- 1/4 cup chia seeds
- 1 cup coconut milk
- 1/2 cup raspberries (fresh or frozen)
- 1-2 tbsp maple syrup or honey
- Shredded coconut for topping

Instructions:

1. **Mix**: In a bowl or jar, combine chia seeds, coconut milk, raspberries, and sweetener. Stir well to combine.
2. **Refrigerate**: Cover and refrigerate for at least 4 hours or overnight.
3. **Serve**: Top with shredded coconut before serving.

Cinnamon Apple Chia Pudding

Ingredients:

- 1/4 cup chia seeds
- 1 cup almond milk
- 1/2 cup applesauce or finely chopped apple
- 1/2 tsp cinnamon
- 1-2 tbsp maple syrup or honey
- Chopped apple for topping

Instructions:

1. **Mix**: In a bowl or jar, combine chia seeds, almond milk, applesauce, cinnamon, and sweetener. Stir well.
2. **Refrigerate**: Cover and refrigerate for at least 4 hours or overnight.
3. **Serve**: Top with chopped apple before serving.

Mocha Chia Pudding

Ingredients:

- 1/4 cup chia seeds
- 1 cup almond milk
- 1 tbsp instant coffee or espresso powder
- 1 tbsp cocoa powder
- 1-2 tbsp maple syrup or honey
- Dark chocolate shavings for topping

Instructions:

1. **Mix**: In a bowl or jar, combine chia seeds, almond milk, instant coffee, cocoa powder, and sweetener. Stir well until the coffee and cocoa dissolve.
2. **Refrigerate**: Cover and refrigerate for at least 4 hours or overnight.
3. **Serve**: Top with dark chocolate shavings before serving.

Pineapple Coconut Chia Pudding

Ingredients:

- 1/4 cup chia seeds
- 1 cup coconut milk
- 1/2 cup pineapple puree (fresh or frozen)
- 1-2 tbsp maple syrup or honey
- Shredded coconut for topping

Instructions:

1. **Mix**: In a bowl or jar, combine chia seeds, coconut milk, pineapple puree, and sweetener. Stir well.
2. **Refrigerate**: Cover and refrigerate for at least 4 hours or overnight.
3. **Serve**: Top with shredded coconut before serving.

Chia Pudding Parfait with Granola

Ingredients:

- 1/4 cup chia seeds
- 1 cup almond milk
- 1-2 tbsp maple syrup or honey
- Granola
- Fresh berries for topping

Instructions:

1. **Mix**: In a bowl or jar, combine chia seeds, almond milk, and sweetener. Stir well and refrigerate for at least 4 hours or overnight.
2. **Layer**: Once the chia pudding has thickened, layer it with granola and fresh berries in a glass.
3. **Serve**: Serve as a parfait with extra granola and berries on top.

Chocolate Coconut Chia Pudding

Ingredients:

- 1/4 cup chia seeds
- 1 cup coconut milk
- 1 tbsp cocoa powder
- 1-2 tbsp maple syrup or honey
- Shredded coconut for topping

Instructions:

1. **Mix**: In a bowl or jar, combine chia seeds, coconut milk, cocoa powder, and sweetener. Stir well.
2. **Refrigerate**: Cover and refrigerate for at least 4 hours or overnight.
3. **Serve**: Top with shredded coconut before serving.

Almond Joy Chia Pudding

Ingredients:

- 1/4 cup chia seeds
- 1 cup almond milk
- 2 tbsp cocoa powder
- 1 tbsp maple syrup or honey
- 2 tbsp shredded coconut
- 1/4 cup sliced almonds
- Chocolate chips for topping (optional)

Instructions:

1. **Mix**: In a bowl or jar, combine chia seeds, almond milk, cocoa powder, maple syrup, and shredded coconut. Stir well.
2. **Refrigerate**: Cover and refrigerate for at least 4 hours or overnight.
3. **Serve**: Top with sliced almonds and chocolate chips before serving.

Kiwi Lime Chia Pudding

Ingredients:

- 1/4 cup chia seeds
- 1 cup coconut milk
- 2 ripe kiwis, peeled and mashed
- Juice of 1 lime
- 1-2 tbsp maple syrup or honey

Instructions:

1. **Mix**: In a bowl or jar, combine chia seeds, coconut milk, mashed kiwi, lime juice, and sweetener. Stir well.
2. **Refrigerate**: Cover and refrigerate for at least 4 hours or overnight.
3. **Serve**: Serve topped with extra kiwi slices and a lime wedge.

Maple Pecan Chia Pudding

Ingredients:

- 1/4 cup chia seeds
- 1 cup almond milk
- 2 tbsp maple syrup
- 1/4 cup chopped pecans
- 1/2 tsp vanilla extract

Instructions:

1. **Mix**: In a bowl or jar, combine chia seeds, almond milk, maple syrup, vanilla extract, and chopped pecans. Stir well.
2. **Refrigerate**: Cover and refrigerate for at least 4 hours or overnight.
3. **Serve**: Top with extra chopped pecans before serving.

Lemon Poppy Seed Chia Pudding

Ingredients:

- 1/4 cup chia seeds
- 1 cup almond milk
- Zest of 1 lemon
- 1 tbsp lemon juice
- 1 tbsp maple syrup or honey
- 1 tbsp poppy seeds

Instructions:

1. **Mix**: In a bowl or jar, combine chia seeds, almond milk, lemon zest, lemon juice, sweetener, and poppy seeds. Stir well.
2. **Refrigerate**: Cover and refrigerate for at least 4 hours or overnight.
3. **Serve**: Top with extra lemon zest or lemon slices before serving.

Acai Berry Chia Pudding

Ingredients:

- 1/4 cup chia seeds
- 1 cup coconut milk
- 2 tbsp acai powder or acai puree
- 1/2 cup mixed berries (fresh or frozen)
- 1-2 tbsp maple syrup or honey

Instructions:

1. **Mix**: In a bowl or jar, combine chia seeds, coconut milk, acai powder, mixed berries, and sweetener. Stir well.
2. **Refrigerate**: Cover and refrigerate for at least 4 hours or overnight.
3. **Serve**: Top with fresh berries before serving.

Banana Nut Chia Pudding

Ingredients:

- 1/4 cup chia seeds
- 1 cup almond milk
- 1 ripe banana, mashed
- 1/4 cup chopped walnuts
- 1 tsp cinnamon
- 1-2 tbsp maple syrup or honey

Instructions:

1. **Mix**: In a bowl or jar, combine chia seeds, almond milk, mashed banana, cinnamon, and sweetener. Stir well.
2. **Refrigerate**: Cover and refrigerate for at least 4 hours or overnight.
3. **Serve**: Top with chopped walnuts before serving.

Tropical Papaya Chia Pudding

Ingredients:

- 1/4 cup chia seeds
- 1 cup coconut milk
- 1/2 cup papaya, pureed
- 1/2 tsp vanilla extract
- 1-2 tbsp maple syrup or honey
- Pineapple chunks for topping

Instructions:

1. **Mix**: In a bowl or jar, combine chia seeds, coconut milk, papaya puree, vanilla extract, and sweetener. Stir well.
2. **Refrigerate**: Cover and refrigerate for at least 4 hours or overnight.
3. **Serve**: Top with pineapple chunks before serving.

Chocolate Raspberry Chia Pudding

Ingredients:

- 1/4 cup chia seeds
- 1 cup almond milk
- 2 tbsp cocoa powder
- 1/2 cup raspberries (fresh or frozen)
- 1-2 tbsp maple syrup or honey
- Dark chocolate shavings for topping

Instructions:

1. **Mix**: In a bowl or jar, combine chia seeds, almond milk, cocoa powder, maple syrup, and raspberries. Stir well.
2. **Refrigerate**: Cover and refrigerate for at least 4 hours or overnight.
3. **Serve**: Top with dark chocolate shavings before serving.

Mixed Berry Chia Pudding

Ingredients:

- 1/4 cup chia seeds
- 1 cup almond milk
- 1/2 cup mixed berries (fresh or frozen)
- 1 tbsp honey or maple syrup
- 1/2 tsp vanilla extract

Instructions:

1. **Mix**: In a bowl or jar, combine chia seeds, almond milk, mixed berries, honey, and vanilla extract. Stir well.
2. **Refrigerate**: Cover and refrigerate for at least 4 hours or overnight.
3. **Serve**: Top with extra fresh berries before serving.

Coconut Mango Chia Pudding

Ingredients:

- 1/4 cup chia seeds
- 1 cup coconut milk
- 1/2 cup mango, pureed
- 1 tbsp maple syrup or honey
- 1/4 tsp vanilla extract

Instructions:

1. **Mix**: In a bowl or jar, combine chia seeds, coconut milk, mango puree, sweetener, and vanilla extract. Stir well.
2. **Refrigerate**: Cover and refrigerate for at least 4 hours or overnight.
3. **Serve**: Top with shredded coconut before serving.

S'mores Chia Pudding

Ingredients:

- 1/4 cup chia seeds
- 1 cup almond milk
- 1 tbsp cocoa powder
- 1 tbsp maple syrup
- 2 tbsp mini marshmallows
- 2 tbsp graham cracker crumbs
- Chocolate chips for topping

Instructions:

1. **Mix**: In a bowl or jar, combine chia seeds, almond milk, cocoa powder, and maple syrup. Stir well.
2. **Refrigerate**: Cover and refrigerate for at least 4 hours or overnight.
3. **Serve**: Top with mini marshmallows, graham cracker crumbs, and chocolate chips before serving.

Pear Ginger Chia Pudding

Ingredients:

- 1/4 cup chia seeds
- 1 cup coconut milk
- 1 ripe pear, peeled and chopped
- 1/2 tsp fresh ginger, grated
- 1 tbsp maple syrup or honey

Instructions:

1. **Mix**: In a bowl or jar, combine chia seeds, coconut milk, chopped pear, grated ginger, and sweetener. Stir well.
2. **Refrigerate**: Cover and refrigerate for at least 4 hours or overnight.
3. **Serve**: Serve topped with extra pear slices before serving.

Sweet Potato Cinnamon Chia Pudding

Ingredients:

- 1/4 cup chia seeds
- 1 cup almond milk
- 1/2 cup cooked sweet potato, mashed
- 1 tsp cinnamon
- 1 tbsp maple syrup or honey
- 1/2 tsp vanilla extract

Instructions:

1. **Mix**: In a bowl or jar, combine chia seeds, almond milk, mashed sweet potato, cinnamon, maple syrup, and vanilla extract. Stir well.
2. **Refrigerate**: Cover and refrigerate for at least 4 hours or overnight.
3. **Serve**: Top with a sprinkle of cinnamon or nuts before serving.

Peach Chia Pudding with Almonds

Ingredients:

- 1/4 cup chia seeds
- 1 cup almond milk
- 1 ripe peach, diced
- 1 tbsp maple syrup or honey
- 1/4 cup sliced almonds

Instructions:

1. **Mix**: In a bowl or jar, combine chia seeds, almond milk, diced peach, and sweetener. Stir well.
2. **Refrigerate**: Cover and refrigerate for at least 4 hours or overnight.
3. **Serve**: Top with sliced almonds before serving.

Carrot Cake Chia Pudding

Ingredients:

- 1/4 cup chia seeds
- 1 cup almond milk
- 1/2 cup grated carrot
- 1 tsp cinnamon
- 1/2 tsp nutmeg
- 1 tbsp maple syrup or honey
- 1/4 cup chopped walnuts

Instructions:

1. **Mix**: In a bowl or jar, combine chia seeds, almond milk, grated carrot, cinnamon, nutmeg, and sweetener. Stir well.
2. **Refrigerate**: Cover and refrigerate for at least 4 hours or overnight.
3. **Serve**: Top with chopped walnuts before serving.

Raspberry Chia Pudding with Walnuts

Ingredients:

- 1/4 cup chia seeds
- 1 cup almond milk
- 1/2 cup raspberries (fresh or frozen)
- 1 tbsp maple syrup or honey
- 1/4 cup chopped walnuts

Instructions:

1. **Mix**: In a bowl or jar, combine chia seeds, almond milk, raspberries, and sweetener. Stir well.
2. **Refrigerate**: Cover and refrigerate for at least 4 hours or overnight.
3. **Serve**: Top with chopped walnuts before serving.

Tropical Kiwi Chia Pudding

Ingredients:

- 1/4 cup chia seeds
- 1 cup coconut milk
- 1/2 cup pineapple, diced
- 1 kiwi, peeled and sliced
- 1 tbsp honey or maple syrup

Instructions:

1. **Mix**: In a bowl or jar, combine chia seeds, coconut milk, pineapple, kiwi, and sweetener. Stir well.
2. **Refrigerate**: Cover and refrigerate for at least 4 hours or overnight.
3. **Serve**: Top with additional kiwi slices before serving.

Pomegranate Chia Pudding

Ingredients:

- 1/4 cup chia seeds
- 1 cup almond milk
- 1/4 cup pomegranate seeds
- 1 tbsp maple syrup or honey
- 1/2 tsp vanilla extract

Instructions:

1. **Mix**: In a bowl or jar, combine chia seeds, almond milk, pomegranate seeds, maple syrup, and vanilla extract. Stir well.
2. **Refrigerate**: Cover and refrigerate for at least 4 hours or overnight.
3. **Serve**: Garnish with extra pomegranate seeds before serving.

Cashew Butter Chia Pudding

Ingredients:

- 1/4 cup chia seeds
- 1 cup almond milk
- 1 tbsp cashew butter
- 1 tbsp maple syrup or honey
- 1/4 tsp cinnamon

Instructions:

1. **Mix**: In a bowl or jar, combine chia seeds, almond milk, cashew butter, maple syrup, and cinnamon. Stir until the cashew butter is well combined.
2. **Refrigerate**: Cover and refrigerate for at least 4 hours or overnight.
3. **Serve**: Top with chopped nuts or berries before serving.

Lemon Raspberry Chia Pudding

Ingredients:

- 1/4 cup chia seeds
- 1 cup almond milk
- 1/2 cup raspberries (fresh or frozen)
- 1 tbsp lemon juice
- 1 tbsp honey or maple syrup

Instructions:

1. **Mix**: In a bowl or jar, combine chia seeds, almond milk, raspberries, lemon juice, and sweetener. Stir well.
2. **Refrigerate**: Cover and refrigerate for at least 4 hours or overnight.
3. **Serve**: Top with extra raspberries and a lemon zest garnish before serving.

Cinnamon Roll Chia Pudding

Ingredients:

- 1/4 cup chia seeds
- 1 cup almond milk
- 1/2 tsp cinnamon
- 1 tbsp maple syrup or honey
- 1/2 tsp vanilla extract

Instructions:

1. **Mix**: In a bowl or jar, combine chia seeds, almond milk, cinnamon, maple syrup, and vanilla extract. Stir well.
2. **Refrigerate**: Cover and refrigerate for at least 4 hours or overnight.
3. **Serve**: Top with chopped pecans or a sprinkle of cinnamon before serving.

Avocado Chocolate Chia Pudding

Ingredients:

- 1/4 cup chia seeds
- 1 cup almond milk
- 1/2 ripe avocado
- 1 tbsp cocoa powder
- 1 tbsp maple syrup or honey
- 1/2 tsp vanilla extract

Instructions:

1. **Mix**: In a blender, combine avocado, almond milk, cocoa powder, maple syrup, and vanilla extract until smooth. Pour into a bowl or jar, then stir in chia seeds.
2. **Refrigerate**: Cover and refrigerate for at least 4 hours or overnight.
3. **Serve**: Top with chocolate chips or berries before serving.

Pineapple Chia Pudding with Macadamia Nuts

Ingredients:

- 1/4 cup chia seeds
- 1 cup coconut milk
- 1/2 cup pineapple, diced
- 1 tbsp maple syrup or honey
- 1/4 cup macadamia nuts, chopped

Instructions:

1. **Mix**: In a bowl or jar, combine chia seeds, coconut milk, pineapple, and maple syrup. Stir well.
2. **Refrigerate**: Cover and refrigerate for at least 4 hours or overnight.
3. **Serve**: Top with chopped macadamia nuts before serving.

Watermelon Mint Chia Pudding

Ingredients:

- 1/4 cup chia seeds
- 1 cup coconut milk
- 1/2 cup watermelon, diced and pureed
- 1 tbsp honey or maple syrup
- 2-3 fresh mint leaves, chopped

Instructions:

1. **Mix**: In a bowl or jar, combine chia seeds, coconut milk, watermelon puree, sweetener, and chopped mint. Stir well.
2. **Refrigerate**: Cover and refrigerate for at least 4 hours or overnight.
3. **Serve**: Top with extra mint leaves before serving.

Coffee Chia Pudding

Ingredients:

- 1/4 cup chia seeds
- 1 cup almond milk (or milk of your choice)
- 1/2 cup brewed coffee (cooled)
- 1 tbsp maple syrup or honey
- 1/2 tsp vanilla extract

Instructions:

1. **Mix**: In a bowl or jar, combine chia seeds, almond milk, cooled coffee, maple syrup, and vanilla extract. Stir well to combine.
2. **Refrigerate**: Cover and refrigerate for at least 4 hours or overnight.
3. **Serve**: Garnish with a sprinkle of cocoa powder or chocolate shavings before serving.

Papaya Lime Chia Pudding

Ingredients:

- 1/4 cup chia seeds
- 1 cup coconut milk
- 1/2 cup papaya, diced
- 1 tbsp lime juice
- 1 tbsp honey or maple syrup

Instructions:

1. **Mix**: In a bowl or jar, combine chia seeds, coconut milk, papaya, lime juice, and sweetener. Stir well.
2. **Refrigerate**: Cover and refrigerate for at least 4 hours or overnight.
3. **Serve**: Top with extra lime zest or papaya slices before serving.

Chocolate Cherry Chia Pudding

Ingredients:

- 1/4 cup chia seeds
- 1 cup almond milk (or milk of your choice)
- 2 tbsp cocoa powder
- 1/4 cup cherries, pitted and chopped
- 1 tbsp maple syrup or honey
- 1/2 tsp vanilla extract

Instructions:

1. **Mix**: In a bowl or jar, combine chia seeds, almond milk, cocoa powder, cherries, maple syrup, and vanilla extract. Stir well until combined.
2. **Refrigerate**: Cover and refrigerate for at least 4 hours or overnight.
3. **Serve**: Top with extra cherries or chocolate chips before serving.

Apple Cinnamon Chia Pudding

Ingredients:

- 1/4 cup chia seeds
- 1 cup almond milk
- 1/2 apple, grated or chopped
- 1/2 tsp cinnamon
- 1 tbsp maple syrup or honey

Instructions:

1. **Mix**: In a bowl or jar, combine chia seeds, almond milk, apple, cinnamon, and maple syrup. Stir well.
2. **Refrigerate**: Cover and refrigerate for at least 4 hours or overnight.
3. **Serve**: Garnish with extra cinnamon or chopped apple before serving.

Spiced Pear Chia Pudding

Ingredients:

- 1/4 cup chia seeds
- 1 cup almond milk (or milk of your choice)
- 1/2 pear, diced
- 1/2 tsp ground ginger
- 1/2 tsp cinnamon
- 1 tbsp maple syrup or honey

Instructions:

1. **Mix**: In a bowl or jar, combine chia seeds, almond milk, pear, ginger, cinnamon, and maple syrup. Stir well.
2. **Refrigerate**: Cover and refrigerate for at least 4 hours or overnight.
3. **Serve**: Top with additional diced pear or a sprinkle of cinnamon before serving.

Blueberry Peach Chia Pudding

Ingredients:

- 1/4 cup chia seeds
- 1 cup almond milk (or milk of your choice)
- 1/2 cup blueberries
- 1/2 peach, diced
- 1 tbsp honey or maple syrup
- 1/2 tsp vanilla extract

Instructions:

1. **Mix**: In a bowl or jar, combine chia seeds, almond milk, blueberries, peach, honey, and vanilla extract. Stir well to combine.
2. **Refrigerate**: Cover and refrigerate for at least 4 hours or overnight.
3. **Serve**: Top with extra fresh fruit or a drizzle of honey before serving.

Cacao Mint Chia Pudding

Ingredients:

- 1/4 cup chia seeds
- 1 cup coconut milk (or milk of your choice)
- 2 tbsp cacao powder
- 1/2 tsp peppermint extract
- 1 tbsp maple syrup or honey

Instructions:

1. **Mix**: In a bowl or jar, combine chia seeds, coconut milk, cacao powder, peppermint extract, and maple syrup. Stir well until smooth.
2. **Refrigerate**: Cover and refrigerate for at least 4 hours or overnight.
3. **Serve**: Top with fresh mint leaves or chocolate shavings before serving.

Goji Berry Chia Pudding

Ingredients:

- 1/4 cup chia seeds
- 1 cup almond milk (or milk of your choice)
- 2 tbsp dried goji berries
- 1 tbsp honey or maple syrup
- 1/2 tsp vanilla extract

Instructions:

1. **Mix**: In a bowl or jar, combine chia seeds, almond milk, goji berries, honey, and vanilla extract. Stir well.
2. **Refrigerate**: Cover and refrigerate for at least 4 hours or overnight.
3. **Serve**: Top with more goji berries or fresh fruit before serving.

Hazelnut Chocolate Chia Pudding

Ingredients:

- 1/4 cup chia seeds
- 1 cup almond milk (or milk of your choice)
- 2 tbsp cacao powder
- 2 tbsp hazelnut butter
- 1 tbsp maple syrup or honey
- 1/2 tsp vanilla extract

Instructions:

1. **Mix**: In a bowl or jar, combine chia seeds, almond milk, cacao powder, hazelnut butter, maple syrup, and vanilla extract. Stir well to combine.
2. **Refrigerate**: Cover and refrigerate for at least 4 hours or overnight.
3. **Serve**: Garnish with chopped hazelnuts or chocolate chips before serving.

Fig and Walnut Chia Pudding

Ingredients:

- 1/4 cup chia seeds
- 1 cup coconut milk (or milk of your choice)
- 2 figs, chopped
- 1/4 cup walnuts, chopped
- 1 tbsp honey or maple syrup
- 1/2 tsp cinnamon

Instructions:

1. **Mix**: In a bowl or jar, combine chia seeds, coconut milk, figs, walnuts, honey, and cinnamon. Stir well to combine.
2. **Refrigerate**: Cover and refrigerate for at least 4 hours or overnight.
3. **Serve**: Top with extra chopped figs or walnuts before serving.

www.ingramcontent.com/pod-product-compliance
Source LLC
TN
1333060526
LV00055B/2610